Microsoft
exp

Other Titles of Interest

Microsoft Outlook 2000 explained

David Weale

Bernard Babani (Publishing) Ltd
The Grampians
Shepherds Bush Road
London W6 7NF
England
www.babanibooks.com

Please Note

Although every care has been taken with the production of this book to ensure that any instructions or any of the other contents operate in a correct and safe manner, the Author and the Publishers do not accept any responsibility for any failure, damage, or loss caused by following the said contents. The Author and Publisher do not take any responsibility for errors or omissions.

The Author and Publisher make no warranty or representation, either express or implied, with respect to the contents of this book, its quality, merchantability or fitness for a particular purpose.

The Author and Publisher will not be liable to the purchaser or to any other person or legal entity with respect to any liability, loss or damage (whether direct, indirect, special, incidental or consequential) caused or alleged to be caused directly or indirectly by this book.

The book is sold as is, without any warranty of any kind, either expressed or implied, respecting the contents, including but not limited to implied warranties regarding the book's quality, performance, correctness or fitness for any particular purpose.

No part of this book may be reproduced or copied by any means whatever without written permission of the publisher.

Preface

Welcome to Microsoft® Outlook™ 2000.

I wrote this book to help you in learning how to use Outlook™ 2000. It is intended to explain the program in a way that I hope you will find useful.

Each section of the book covers a different aspect of the program and contains various hints and tips which I have found useful and may enhance your work.

The text is written both for the new user and for the more experienced person who wants an easy to follow reference.

Please note that you should know how to use the basic techniques of Microsoft® Windows® 98; if you do not, there are many excellent texts on the subject.

I hope you learn from this book and have fun doing so.

Best wishes,

David Weale January 2001

Trademarks

About the author

David Weale is a Fellow of the Institute of Chartered Accountants and has worked in both private and public practice. At present, he is a lecturer in business computing.

Contents

Starting Off

The screen

Once Outlook has been installed, the initial program screen (which is the one you will see whenever you start the program) will be displayed.

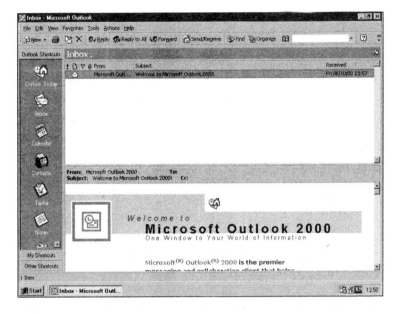

The message from Microsoft is worth reading and then you may want to delete it or store it in a separate folder.

What the screen shows

Outlook, like all Microsoft programs can be customized to reflect the way you work. You can display various toolbars and choose between different screen layouts. These will all be covered within the text.

The initial screen contains the main elements and you may find that this is perfectly suitable for your needs.

> The contents of the toolbars will change depending upon which folder you are currently looking in.

Tip
Often, only the buttons you use are displayed within a toolbar, clicking the **More** Button can access the other available buttons.

Common **Windows** buttons such as **Cut, Paste** and so on are not covered within this text as it is assumed the reader will be familiar with their use.

The three Shortcut bars (on the left of the screen) are **Outlook Shortcuts**, **My Shortcuts** and **Other Shortcuts**.

Tips

Moving the mouse pointer (so it becomes a double-headed arrow) onto the divide between sections, clicking, and dragging the divider will alter the relative size of any of the sections of the screen.

Remember that you can use the **right** button on your mouse to display a menu (the contents of which apply to your current activity). This is a quicker way of carrying out common tasks.

If you look closely at many of the individual screens, you can see that many of the data fields have an **arrow** to the right (which pulls down a list from which you can select). Alternatively, there may be several dots to the right of the field name or menu item, this means there are further choices.

Outlook Shortcuts

This contains the most used shortcuts (by clicking the shortcut you can access the folder or file more quickly).

Tip
These can be viewed as large buttons or small ones. **Right** click with the mouse pointer within the Shortcut Bar to alternate between large and small buttons.

My Shortcuts

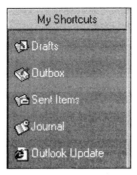

This contains the buttons for activities you use less often, remember you can move shortcuts from one bar to another, add shortcuts or delete them (from any shortcut bar).

Other Shortcuts

These link to folders on your (hard) disc.

Working with the shortcut bars

The buttons on the shortcut bars are those that you will use most (assuming you work in the way Microsoft intend), however you can make changes to this.

You can add to or remove any shortcut on any of the shortcut bars.

Adding Shortcuts
To do so, within the Outlook Bar you want to add the shortcut to, **right** click the mouse. Next, select **Outlook Bar Shortcut** from the menu and choose the folder you want to add to the Outlook Bar. It will then appear as an additional button.

Adding Groups
You can also add a new Shortcut Bar (in additional to the **Outlook**, **My** and **Other** Shortcut Bars) using the same technique but this time selecting **Add New Group** from the menu).

Moving Shortcuts within a shortcut bar
Click and drag the shortcut to a new position (you will see a line appear between the buttons as you move down the bar) release the mouse button when it is in the correct position.

Moving Shortcuts to another shortcut bar

Click and drag the shortcut to another shortcut bar (you have to drag it to the title of the bar and then wait for the bar to open before dragging it to the position within the bar where you want it to appear).

Removing shortcuts/groups

Right click the shortcut or group title and select the **Remove** option.

Using the Shortcuts

Outlook Today

This view can be used to look at the day's activities, appointments, tasks, and e-mail messages.

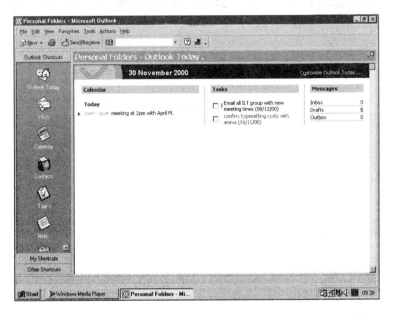

This can be set to appear as the default view (the first screen you see). To do this, select **Outlook Today** and then the **Customize Outlook Today** button (top right hand of the window).

In the **Startup** section, click the **When starting, go directly to Outlook Today** box so that it has a tick and then **Save Changes**.

You can make various other changes to the way in which the **Outlook Today** view is shown on the screen (in order to reflect your methods of work). The screen is shown below for reference.

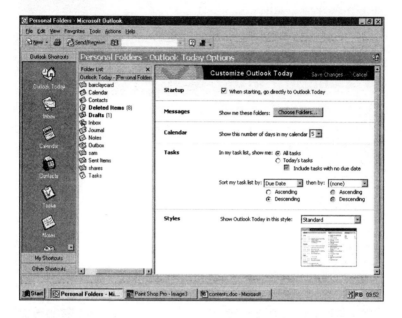

Messages

By default, your mail arrives in your **Inbox** folder and **Outlook Today** displays this.

If you have filtered the mail to arrive in different folders (create a **Rule** to do this) then you can set these to appear in **Outlook Today** using the **Choose Folders** button.

Inbox

The default view (the view you get when you start the program), this shows the mail you have received.

Working with your Inbox

The Inbox shows the mail you have received, you can alter the way in which it is sorted by clicking any of the column headings e.g. **Subject**.

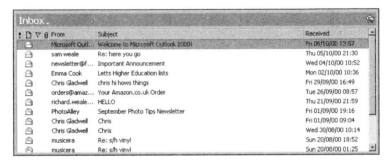

Sorting by Icons

♦	The importance of the message, 🔺 = high importance and ♦ denotes low importance – these symbols can be added to a message when you create it
🗋	Sort by the type of file
▽	Flag status, you can add a flag to an outgoing message, so that you can check if the message has been followed up.
🔗	This shows if a file has been attached to the message, normally any attachment can be opened in the originating program by double-clicking the attachment symbol.

Tips

If you want to keep a message but not to show it in the **Inbox** then move it to another folder (see **View**, **Folder List**), or you can delete it by highlighting the message and using the **delete** key.

You can automatically re-route incoming e-mail by creating a **Rule** to place the message in a different folder (from the Inbox).

Viewing attachments

The contents of the selected (highlighted) message are shown in the **Preview Pane** (below the list of messages). To open an attachment, you can double-click the attachment symbol (on the right of the illustration below) and select the attachment you want to open, which will be opened in its originating program, e.g. Word.

To view a message in its own window, double-click the selected message.

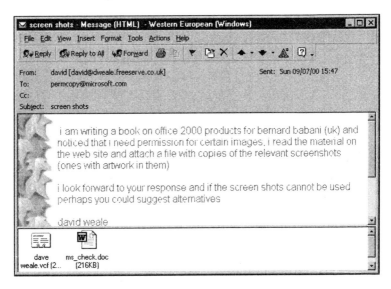

The attachments are now shown below the message and will open if they are double-clicked.

The Inbox toolbar

This toolbar assists you in dealing with your incoming mail (**Find** and **Organize** are dealt with in a separate section as they appear on all the toolbars).

New

You can start a new message (see section on **New Messages**).

Print

Print the message.

Move

Move it to a new folder, this pulls down a list of the folders (including those you have created).

Delete

Clicking this deletes the selected messages and moves them to the **Deleted Items** folder.

Reply (Reply to All)

Reply to the sender (**Reply**) or to the sender and those in the **To** and **CC** sections of the original message (**Reply to All**).

Forward

Forward the message to someone else, you can add text to the message before you send it (if you wish).

The message is then shown with a new icon to show it has been forwarded.

Send/Receive

Phones your ISP and sends all unsent messages while collecting your post and downloading it onto your computer.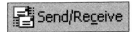

New Messages

To create a new message, you can click the **New** button *or* click the arrow to the right, which pulls down the menu shown below.

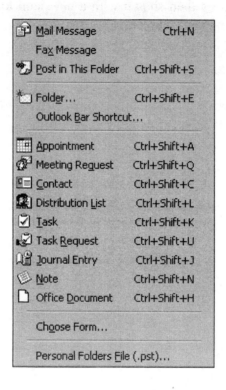

Mail Message

If you click the **New** button or select **Mail Message** from the menu, you will begin the process of creating a new e-mail message and the following window will appear.

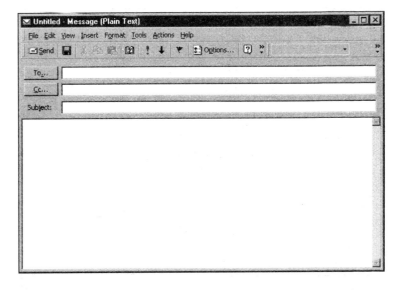

To:

You can type an e-mail address in this box, or if you click on the **To** button, your address book will be displayed.

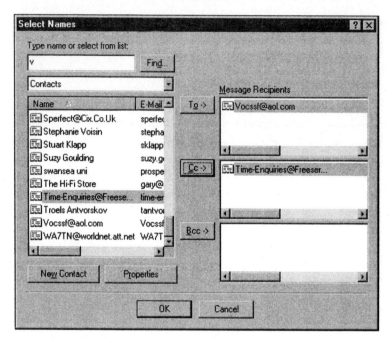

Tip

If you type a letter or part of a name in the **Find** box then the program will move to that part of the address list.

Tips

You **must** click the **To**, **Cc** buttons, etc., to ensure that the e-mail is sent somewhere, mail will only be sent to people whose addresses appear in the **Message Recipients** boxes.

Any number of e-mail addresses can be included in the **Message Recipients** boxes.

Subject

Always include a subject in any e-mail message, it is much easier for the recipient if you do (they have an idea of the contents of the message), it is also good manners.

Finally, enter the text of your message in the main section of the box.

Changing the font for messages

You can only change the font for messages if you change the setting from **Plain Text** (**Tools, Options, Mail Format**).

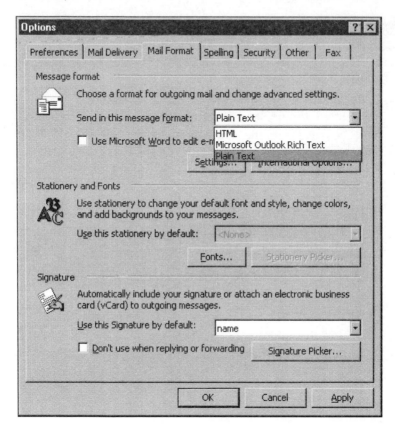

The toolbar buttons

The exact order and the actual buttons displayed depends upon your use of them, if you use the **More** button and then use the additional buttons that appear, these will then be displayed on the toolbar next time you use the program.

Send

This sends your message (if you are not connected to the Internet then the message will be saved in the **Outbox** – to see the contents of the **Outbox**, select **My Shortcuts**).

Save

Saves the file (in the **My Documents** folder), you can save it elsewhere by pulling down the **File** menu and selecting **Save As**.

Address Book

Displays the address book. You can add to the e-mail addresses, delete them, and edit them.

Flags and Importance Levels

You can set importance levels and a flag to your messages ▪ = high importance and ↓ denotes low importance.

Flag status, you can add a flag to an outgoing message, this is to set a flag so that you can check if the message has been followed up.

Options

You can alter various settings for your mail.

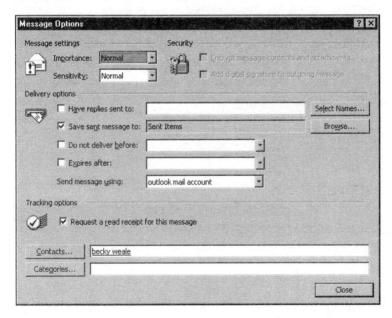

For example, it may be useful to tick the box **Request a read receipt for the message**, note that this will *only* affect those contacts or categories you have selected using the buttons in the **Tracking options** section.

More buttons
There are further buttons available by clicking this.

Signature
You can add a prepared signature to your e-mail by selecting from the list.

Creating a signature
To create new signatures or to remove existing signatures, you need to pull down the **Tools** menu (main Outlook screen), select **Options** followed by **Mail Format** and **Signature Picker**.

If you choose to use a specific signature by default then it will appear automatically in any message (**Use this Signature by default**).

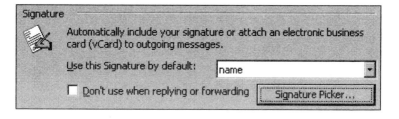

Tip
You will not be able to change the font unless you have changed the message format from **Plain Text** (**Tools**, **Options**, **Mail Format**).

Attachments

It is often necessary to attach a file (text or picture) to an e-mail; thus, you can send any file (although there may be constraints on the size of the file) with your e-mail message.

To add an attachment, click the button and select the file you want to attach (from anywhere on your system).

Normally any attachment can be opened in the originating program by double-clicking it (you can use this technique to check that you have included the correct attachment).

Check Names

Click this button to check names you type in the **To** box, a correct address will be underlined (or if the address is not found you can create a **New Contact** and add the address to your address book).

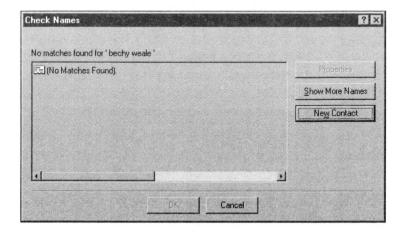

If there is more than one address, you choose from the list.

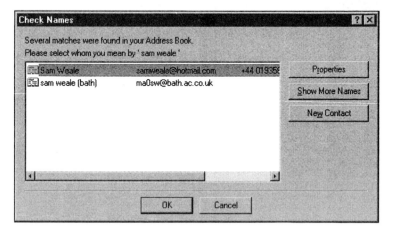

Reading your e-mail

Make sure you looking at your **Inbox** (or the folder your e-mail is stored in if you have changed this) and double click the message to read it.

You can then reply (or forward) to the message by clicking on the relevant button on the toolbar.

When you use the **Reply** button to reply to a message, the original message is shown below the reply, the idea being to maintain the thread of the conversation.

AutoPreview

Pull down the **View** menu and select **AutoPreview**; the **Inbox** will now display the first three lines of the e-mail message (as opposed to just the subject and sender).

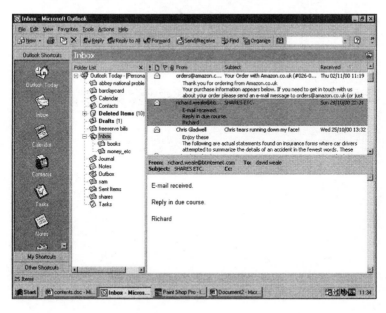

Deleting messages

Select the message(s); press the **Delete** key on the keyboard or the toolbar button.

To permanently delete items, click on the **Deleted Items** button with the **right mouse button**, select **Empty "Deleted Items" Folder** and confirm the deletion (or to select individual items for permanent deletion, select the items and **right click** the mouse and confirm the deletion, to select all the items you can pull down the **Edit** menu and then **Select All**).

Restoring deleted items

Select the **Deleted Items** button (Outlook Shortcuts bar) and then select the item you want to restore, drag it to any of the folders shown, e.g. the **Inbox**.

Tips

It can be useful to display the **Folder List** (**View** menu and **Folder List**) at this stage so you can see all the folders.

Remember that folders with a ⊞ to the left of the folder name contain sub-folders which can be displayed by clicking on the ⊞ (which then becomes a ⊟).

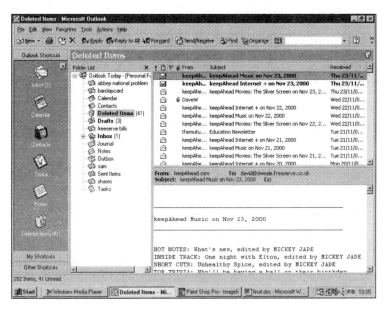

Calendar

The Calendar enables you to manage your time, appointments and other activities. You can also use it in conjunction with the calendars of other people to arrange meetings.

You can view a day at a time, or a week or a month; the default is the daily view.

The default screen is shown below.

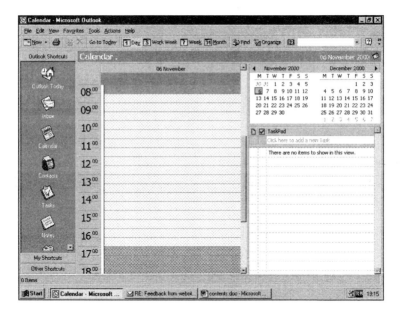

The buttons along the top of the screen enable you to show different views of the calendar, for example the **7 day** week is shown below.

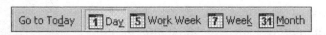

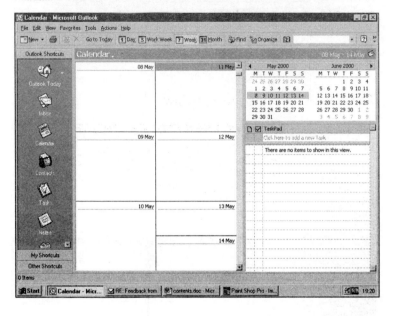

Altering the view

There are several ways of viewing the calendar. To alter the view, pull down the **View** menu and select **Current View**.

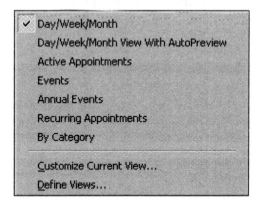

The **Active Appointments** view is shown here.

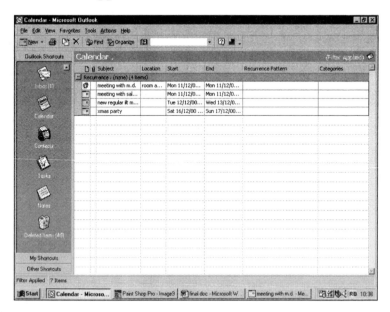

Creating an appointment or meeting

To enter an item, click in the space for that date and type in the entry.

Double-click the entry to edit or add details. For example, if you remove the tick for **All day event** then you will be able to allocate a time to it.

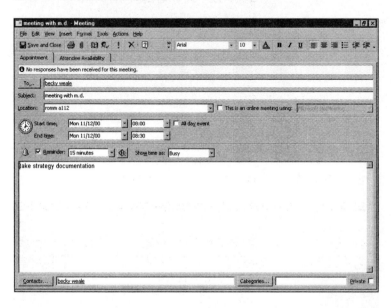

You can attach a file (e.g. an agenda) to a meeting request as an attachment.

Blocks of time

Click and drag the mouse to select a block of time within the calendar and then **right click** (with the mouse) and select from the choice of activities. This allocates that block of time to the chosen activity.

Attendee Availability

When you are editing the calendar item (by double clicking the item), as well as editing, you can invite people to attend the meeting or other appointment by moving to the **Attendee Availability** screen, add them to the list (using the **Invite Others** button) and you can e-mail with details of the meeting using the **Send** button.

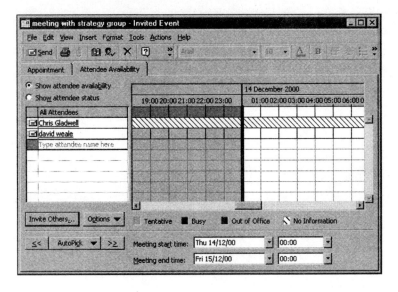

Recurring Appointments/Events

If an event is regular, you can automatically set it to appear in the calendar.

Open an event by double-clicking it within the calendar and pull down the **Actions** menu, select **Recurrence** and fill in the details.

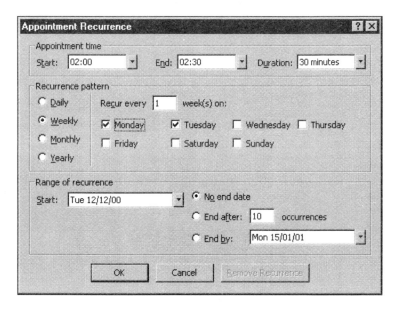

Altering Appointments or Meetings

Double click the item and make any changes you wish, **Save and Close**. If you have e-mailed the participants then you will be asked if you want to send updates.

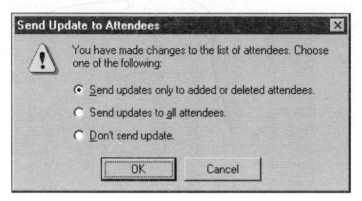

To remove participants, select the person and press the **delete** button on the toolbar. You will be prompted to send a cancellation notice (if you notified them initially).

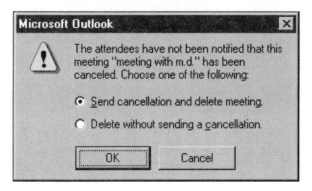

Deleting a Meeting

Select the meeting and click the **delete** button on the toolbar.

Normally an e-mail will be sent to the invited participants cancelling the meeting and any resources will be freed up.

Contacts

Keeps a record of people's addresses, Internet URLs, and any other information you want to record about each individual contact.

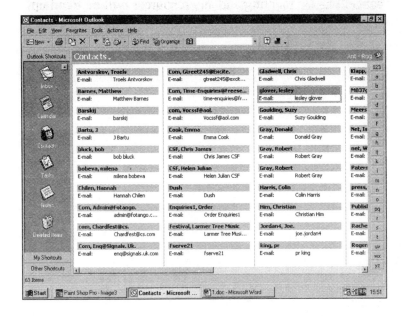

Looking at your contacts (different views)

If you pull down the **View** menu (top of screen), and then select **Current View**, you will see that you have a choice of ways in which you can look at the contacts.

For example, **Detailed Address Cards** gives more detail than **Address Cards**.

If you double click the contact details (in any view) you can bring up the original data entry screens so that you can add to or alter the data.

Autodialling Contacts

You may be able to automatically dial contacts
(depending upon your telephone system), select
the contact then click the arrow to the right of
the **AutoDial** button on the toolbar and select
the number to call.

Alternatively, click the **AutoDial** button itself and the
following dialog box will appear (you can change the
number by pulling down the list of numbers in the number
box).

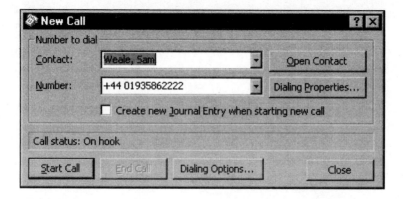

Click the **Start Call** button, make the call, and then click
the **End Call** button.

If you tick the box **Create new Journal Entry when starting new call** then once you begin to dial by clicking the **Start Call** button, a new journal is displayed so that you can add notes recording the contents of the conversation.

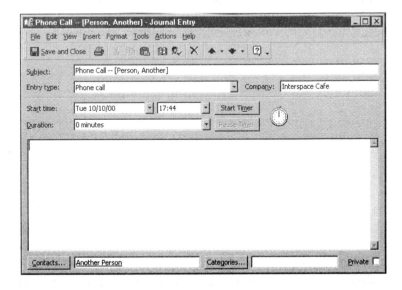

Looking at your contacts web pages

Assuming you have entered the URL into the contact information and that you are on-line, then you can view the web site by clicking on the web site address (within the detailed screen obtained by double-clicking the contacts details).

Individual Contacts

When you double-click a contact, you obtain the details of the contact, which you can add to or edit. There are several tabs on this screen, which are worth exploring, as well as a rather interesting new button.

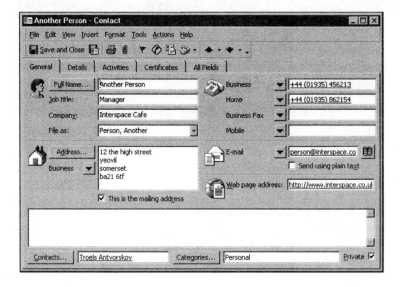

Display Map of Address

If you click this button, you will be connected to the Internet web site for **Expedia.com** and will be able to look at a map of the surrounding area where the contact has an address.

General/Details

These contain the data fields into which you enter any details you want to record about the contact.

Activities

If you click this tab, a list of all the activities (for that contact) will be displayed.

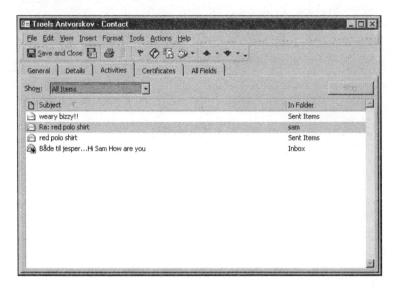

You can show **All Items** (as above) or pull down the list and select the particular item you are interested in tracking for that contact.

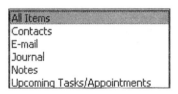

Tasks

Use **Tasks** to set and track an activity through from start to finish.

You can set up single or recurring tasks (e.g. you need to send a leaflet to everyone on your mailing list).

You can open existing tasks using either the **Task** or **Calendar** view buttons (the **TaskPad** is shown on the right side of the **Calendar** screen).

Creating tasks

Click the **New** button or pull down the **File** menu; select **New**, and then **Task**.

In the **Subject** box, give the task a name and select the options you want.

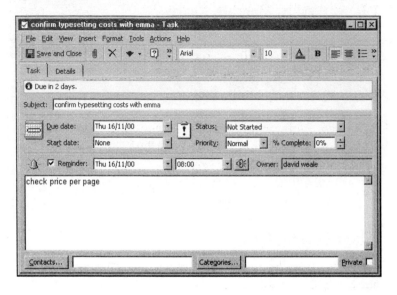

If you want to set a repeated task, pull down the **Actions** menu and select **Recurrence** and then how often it recurs **(Daily, Weekly, Monthly, Yearly)**.

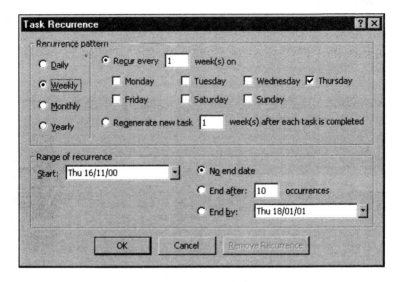

If you want a recurring task to start and end on specific dates, set start and end dates, select **Regenerate new task**, and enter how frequently the task should recur.

Task Requests

Open a task and click the **Assign Task** button.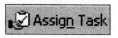

In the **To** box, enter the name of the person you want to assign the task to or use the **To** button to select from the list of contacts. Set the other options as you wish.

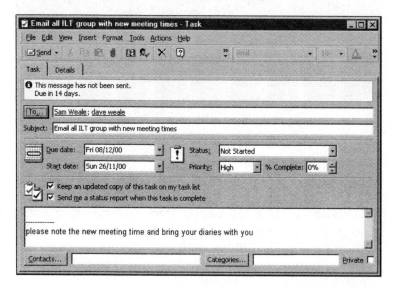

The text box is intended for you to type any additional information about the task that would be useful to you or the person assigned the task.

Finally, **Send** the task to the assignee.

Altering the look of tasks

To change the colour of overdue or completed tasks, pull down the **Tools** menu, select **Options**, then **Preferences**, and finally, **Task Options**.

Choose a colour in the **Overdue tasks** box and the **Completed tasks** box.

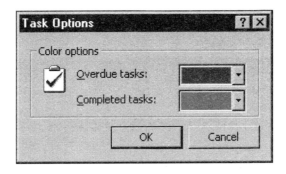

Sorting and grouping tasks

Use **Current View**, and then select **Customize Current View**. Choose **Sort** or **Group By**.

Sequencing tasks

You can drag a task up or down in the task list, using the mouse.

Notes

The Outlook version of sticky paper notes, you can write notes to remind yourself of thoughts, ideas, memos you need to write and so on.

They are certainly an alternative to leaving sticky bits of paper on your desk or computer screen.

Creating notes

Pull down the **New** button arrow and select **Note**. Enter your text and you have a note.

You can move the note around the screen by clicking and dragging it.

Opening a note

Select the **Notes** view button and then double-click the note you want to look at. You can change the contents, and they will be saved automatically.

Changing the look of a note

You can alter the colour of a note by clicking the icon in the top left of the note and selecting **Color** from the menu, notes are by default yellow simply because that is the usual colour.

The colour and format of the text and note can also be changed by pulling down the **Tools** menu, selecting **Options**, and the **Preferences** tab. Finally, select **Note Options** and make your desired changes.

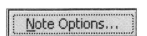

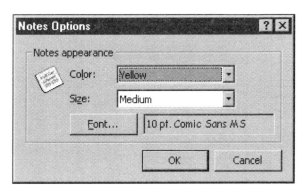

Displaying the time and date on notes

The date and time may show in the bottom left of the note, if you want to remove these, pull down the **Tools** menu, select **Options**, then **Other**, and finally **Advanced Options**.

Select or remove the tick on **When viewing Notes, show time, and date**.

Deleting notes

Select the note (**Notes** view button) and either use the keyboard **delete** or the **Delete** button on the toolbar.

Adding notes to messages

You can incorporate the notes into messages, etc., by selecting the note, clicking the **Copy** button, moving to the message and then **Paste** the note (if you position the cursor in the body text section of the message, it will be included as an attachment).

Tip

If the copy and paste buttons are not displayed you can use the keyboard shortcuts (**Ctrl C** to copy and **Ctrl V** to paste, hold down the **Ctrl** key while pressing the other key) or pull down the **Edit** menu.

Deleted Items

This button shows the messages that you have deleted; they are stored in this folder until you delete them permanently.

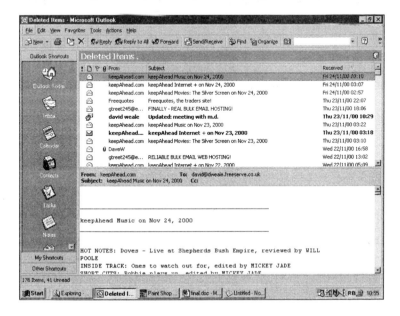

Permanently deleting items

To delete them permanently, highlight them and either select the **Delete** button or the **delete** key; there is a further on-screen prompt to ensure you do not accidentally delete items.

The list can be sorted by clicking the column headings.

Tip

You can highlight all the messages by pulling down the **Edit** menu and choosing **Select All**.

You can achieve the same result by holding down the **Shift** key and clicking the mouse on the first and then last item, you want to select.

Alternatively, holding down the **Ctrl** key and clicking on each message you want to choose allows you to select non-sequential items.

My Shortcuts

Drafts

Messages that you have begun and then saved (but not sent) will be stored in this folder.

To edit or carry on with the message, double-click it in the **Drafts** folder and carry on.

When you click the **Send** button, it will move from this folder to either the **Outbox** or **Sent Items** folders depending upon whether you are connected to the Internet at the time.

Outbox

It is usual to compose messages while off-line (not connected to the Internet).

If you click the **Send/Receive** button, the message will be moved to the **Outbox** and will be sent (and moved to the **Sent Items** folder) when you connect to the Internet and send it using the **Send/Receive** button.

Sent Items

All the messages you have sent are stored in this folder.

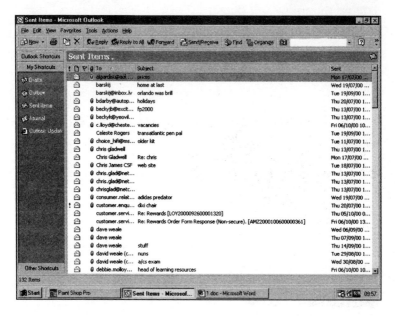

You can remove old messages by selecting them and either clicking the **Delete** button or using the **delete** key on the keyboard. The deleted messages are sent to the **Deleted Items** folder.

You can sort the folder by clicking the column headings.

Journal

This can be used to track documents and e-mails. You can automatically record (track) the following items:

❖ E-mail messages

❖ Meeting requests

❖ Meeting responses

❖ Meeting cancellations

❖ Task requests

❖ Task responses

Documents created in the following programs can be automatically recorded in the Journal:

❖ Microsoft Access

❖ Microsoft Excel

❖ Microsoft PowerPoint

❖ Microsoft Word

You can look at the **Journal** using different views (**View** menu followed by **Current View**).

The following two illustrations show **Contact** view (the items are categorised by contact and by time (there is a timeline along the top of the screen) and by **Type**.

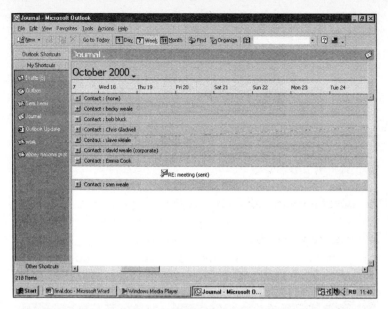

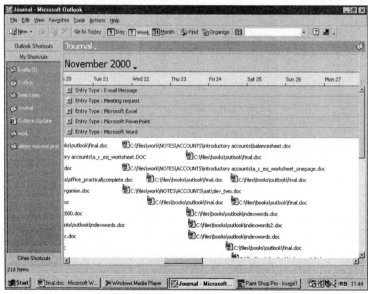

Recording journal entries

To record items automatically in the journal, pull down the **Tools** menu, then click **Options** and after selecting the **Preferences** tab, click **Journal Options** (this button appears in the **Contacts** section of the dialog box).

Journal Options...

In the **Automatically record these items** box, check the relevant items you want automatically recorded and in the **For these contacts** box and the **Also record files from** box, check the boxes for the items you want automatically recorded in the journal.

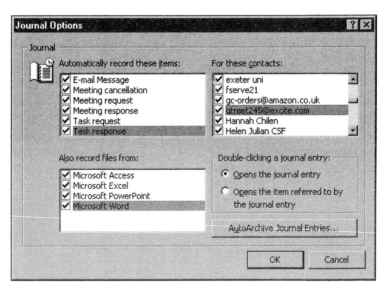

The **AutoArchive Journal Entries** button enables you to clean up the journal by archiving the older items and to choose which folder to archive.

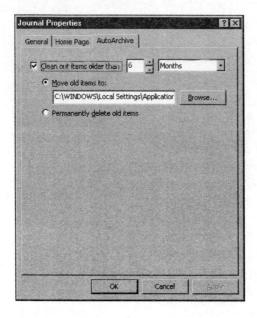

Outlook Update

This will load the Microsoft web site and enable you to download updates and program fixes.

Finding & Organising Items

Find and Organize

You can use **Find** (and **Advanced Find**) to locate items you have received or created using Outlook, and you can use **Organize** to bring structure to the Outlook items you store on your hard disc.

Each of these tools is available from within all the different views, e.g. **Inbox**, **Tasks**, etc., however the options differ depending upon the view.

Find

Enables you to search for a word or phrase (within the items), this is a quick and easy way to find a message especially if the folders are rather full.

Tip
To avoid cluttering your folders (especially your **Inbox**), create **Rules** or use the **Organize** tool to move items to other folders.

Find

If you click the **Find** button on the toolbar, you will see the following screen.

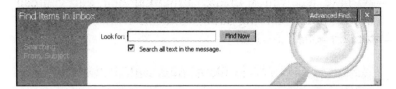

Enter the words or phrase you are looking for and click the **Find Now** button. The messages that contain the text will be shown.

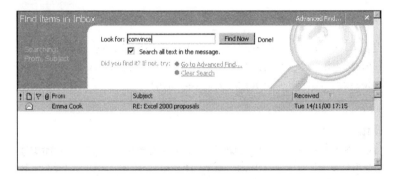

Once the search has been completed, you are offered the choice of **Clear Search** (this removes the text you have entered) or **Go to Advanced Find**.

Tip
The tick in the **Search all text in the message** means that the whole message will be searched, if you remove the tick then only the **From** and **Subject** text will be searched.

Advanced Find

There is an **Advanced Find** that enables you to be more specific and sophisticated in your search parameters. There are three tabs, which you use to narrow your search, this is useful if you have a large number of messages to sort through.

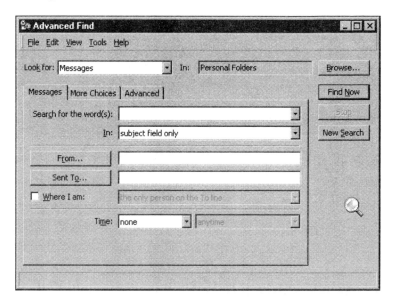

Organize

You can organize the items within Outlook in various ways, within your **Inbox**, **Calendar**, etc. The available options depend upon the folder you are viewing.

Using Folders

You can instruct the program to move incoming messages to a specific folder. The **Move** option moves the selected message(s), however if you create a **Rule** then the message will be moved automatically.

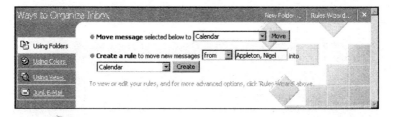

The **Rules Wizard** can be used to set up rules for incoming messages; for example, you could set up a rule to *automatically* forward a message from a person to a specific folder.

Using Colours

You can decide to colour messages **from** or **sent to** a certain source in a different colour.

The **Automatic Formatting** button enables you to set the types of message this applies to.

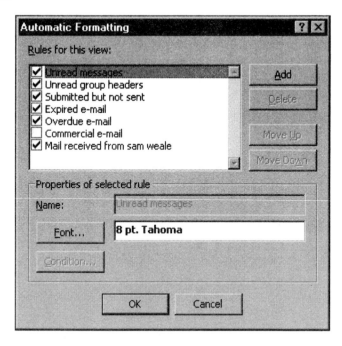

Using Views

By altering the **View**, the items displayed will be changed.
You can see the effect immediately.

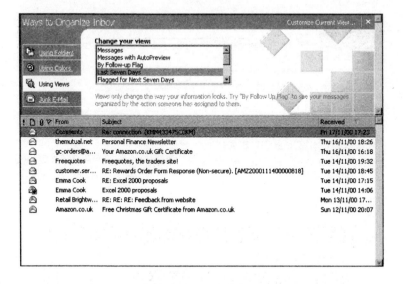

If you click the **Customize Current View** button, you can alter the way the items are displayed by altering the settings within the **View Summary**.

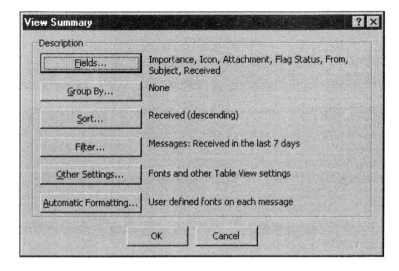

The **View Summary** adds another level of ways of organising the items.

Junk e-mail

This allows you to colour or move junk mail or mail with an adult content.

To actually set the parameters, use the **click here** button to display the choices.

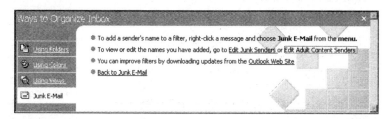

The section on the **Action** menu explains how to add addresses to the **Junk** mail or **Adult Content** lists.

The Menus

The pull-down menus

Each of these is discussed in varying depth, depending upon its relative importance (and whether the topic is covered elsewhere).

File menu

New

This enables you to create new messages and so on, it is an alternative to the **New** button.

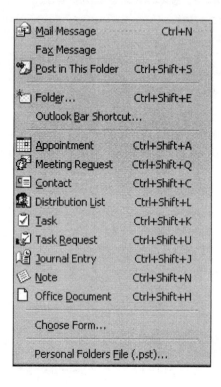

Open

You can open selected (highlighted) items or you can open a **Personal Folder** (you can create a folder anywhere on your hard disc to hold **Outlook** files, these have a **.pst** or **.ost** extension and you can search the hard disc for personal folders using **Advanced Find**).

Personal folders are also shown as buttons within the **My Shortcuts** bar.

Creating a personal folder
On the **Outlook Bar**, click **Other Shortcuts**, then **My Computer**.

Double-click the drive you want the new folder located in and pull down the **File** menu, point to **New**, and then select **Folder**. Finally, type a name for your (new) folder.

> If you want to create a folder within another folder, double-click the folder and proceed as above.

You can add a folder to any of the shortcut bars by clicking and dragging that folder onto the shortcut bar.

Close All Items

This closes all the open windows, e.g. messages, tasks, notes.

Save As

This will save the file, the default location is **My Documents**, it is saved as an **.htm** file although you can choose another format by pulling down the list of file types in the **Save as type** box. This does not save the attachments.

Save Attachments

You can save the attachments using this; you will be given a choice of saving individual attachments or all of them (if there is more than one).

Folder

This option enables you to manage the selected folder, in this illustration the **Sent Items** folder was selected before pulling down the menu.

Share

This is very useful feature as it allows many people to share information and to communicate between themselves using the same folder.

You can share a folder with other people across a network and if you select to do this, there is a wizard, which will assist you in making the correct choices.

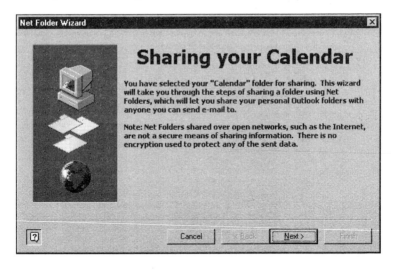

Note the warning about the lack of encryption, any items or data you share across the Internet may not be very secure, and you have to decide if this is acceptable to you.

The next screen asks you to decide whom you want to share the folder with, you select names from your address book.

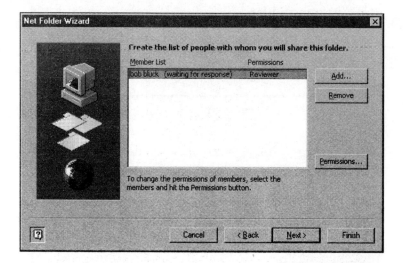

You can select which permissions to allocate to each sharer by using the **Permissions** button.

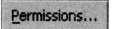

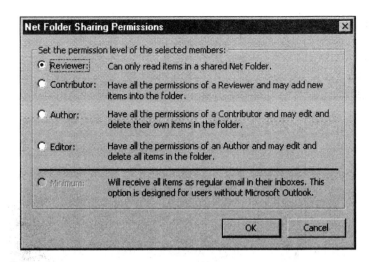

You then give the folder a name (on the next screen) and finally a screen appears which explains that each person you have chosen to share with will be e-mailed with an invitation.

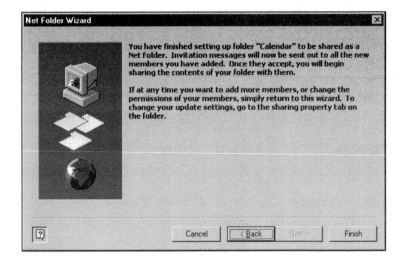

Import and Export

You can import and export from **Outlook**. This is useful and avoids having to enter details (e.g. e-mail addresses) again.

If you have been using **Microsoft Outlook Express** then you can import all the details, settings and data from that program into **Outlook** itself.

The process uses a wizard and leads you step by step, making the necessary choices as you go.

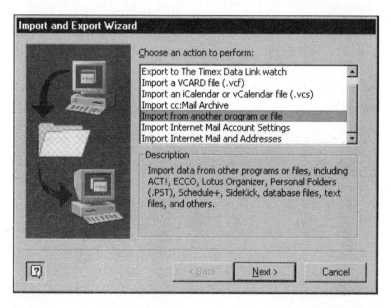

If you are importing from **Outlook Express** (or another popular program), choose the last two items, **Mail Account Settings** and **Mail and Addresses** if you want to use (either of) them in **Outlook** without having to re-enter the data.

On the next screen, you select the program you are importing from and choose the items you wish to import.

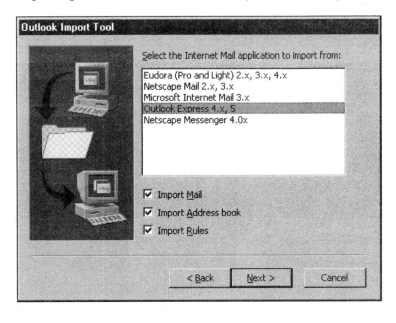

There is a final screen, in which you may want to alter the default settings (in particular the duplicates setting).

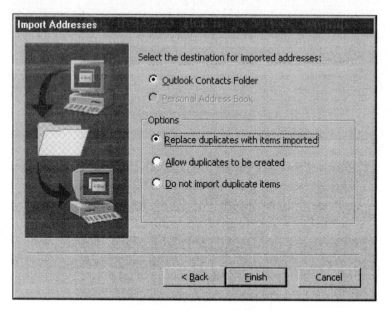

Import Addresses

Select the destination for imported addresses:

- ⦿ Outlook Contacts Folder
- ○ Personal Address Book

Options
- ⦿ Replace duplicates with items imported
- ○ Allow duplicates to be created
- ○ Do not import duplicate items

[< Back] [**Finish**] [Cancel]

Archive

You can archive old items (to avoid having too many items to look at and sort) just as you would store old paper items.

The screen gives you various options for the archiving process.

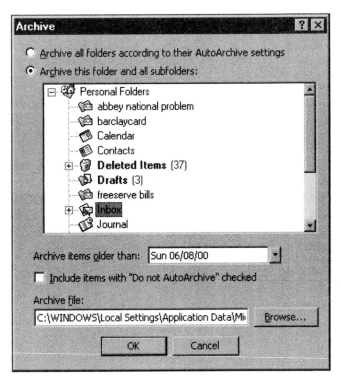

Setting archive properties

You can set archiving properties for each folder by right-clicking it (after selecting the **View** menu and **Folder List**) and selecting **Properties** and **AutoArchive**.

Alternatively, set them globally using the **Tools** menu, **Options**, **Other** and **AutoArchive**.

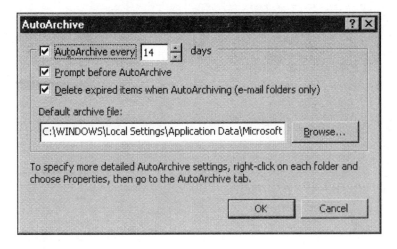

Page Setup/Preview

It is possible to customize the page setup for printing messages.

> The options available depend upon the folder being viewed.

Define Print Styles

Initially you can choose between two layouts.

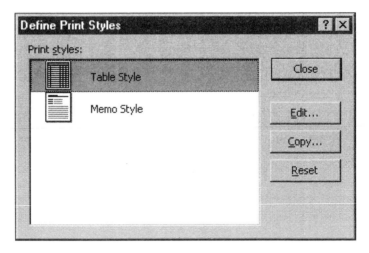

You can edit the layout, copy it, and then change the copy (or the original), fonts, paper size, margins, headers, and footers to customize the printouts (using the buttons shown).

Editing the layout

The options to alter the layout are shown below.

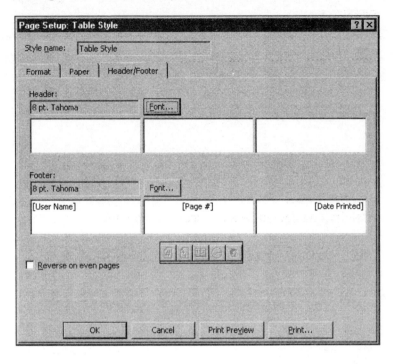

Use the **Print Preview** button to see how the page looks.

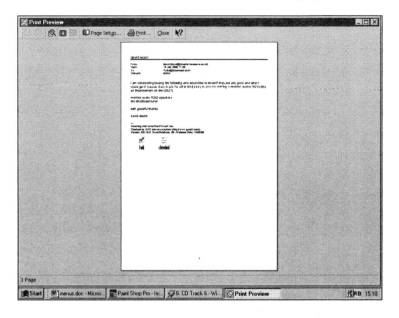

Print

To print, at this stage you can change the **Page Setup**, number of copies and so on.

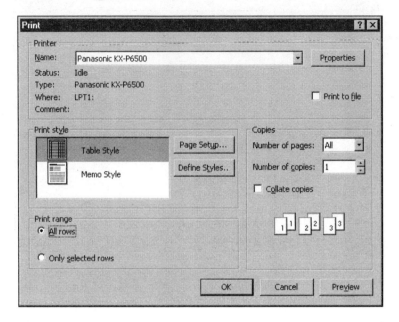

Work Offline

If you select to work offline, Outlook will not automatically send messages (only when you decide to).

Edit menu

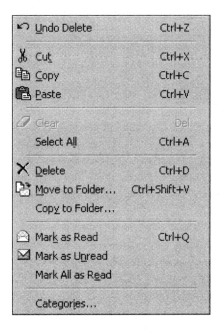

It is assumed that the common activities such as cut and paste, etc., are familiar and have not been dealt with here.

Mark as Read/Unread/All as Read

You can select messages and mark them as read/unread, etc., described by the symbol to the left of the message.

Unread	
Read	
Forwarded or replied to	

Categories

You can use categories to find, sort, filter, or group items within Outlook, for example you can use categories to keep track of items stored in different folders.

If you pull down the **View** menu, (**Current View**) there is a **Category** option, which enables you to quickly view items by category (this is not available for e-mails though).

View menu

The contents of this menu (as with others) will vary depending upon whether you are dealing with e-mail, tasks, etc.

Current View

You can look at the items within Outlook in many different ways, the default is **Messages** (for e-mail activities such as the **Inbox**), but will vary with the activity.

The e-mail choice is shown below for reference.

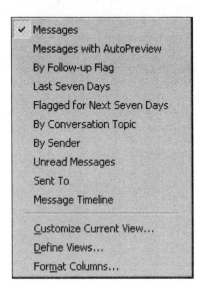

Customize Current View

Click the folder you want to sort, filter, etc.

Pull down the **View** menu, select **Current View**, and then **Customize Current View**.

There is a choice of ways in which you can organize the items.

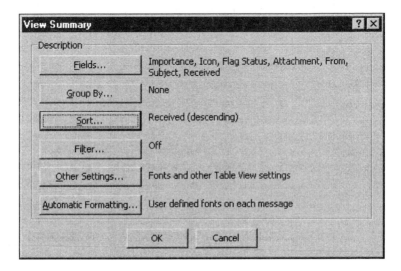

Sort

You can sort the items (remember you can also sort by clicking the column headings for any of the fields).

This method of sorting enables you to sort on multiple fields, for example, you could sort by the date of receipt and within that by the dates they were created.

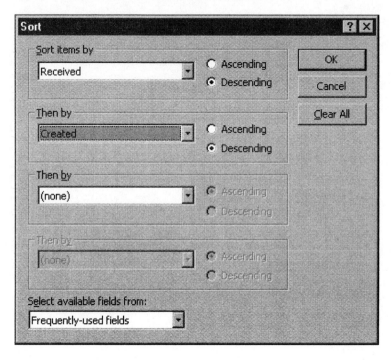

Filter

You can also filter the items; this differs from sorting in that you are making a selection from the complete data. For example, you may only want to show the contacts whose name begins with a certain character.

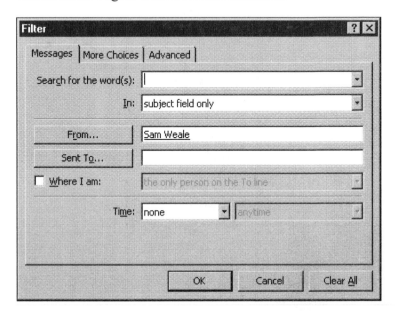

The **Clear All** button removes the filtering.

Go To

Use this to move from one part of the program to another, the list is shown below, however it is often quicker to use the buttons on the left of the screen in the **Outlook Shortcuts**.

Outlook Bar

This toggles the **Outlook Shortcuts Bar** on and off, if it is turned off then the previous command (**Go To**) becomes much more useful.

Folders List

This toggles the **Folders List** on and off. The screen below shows the **Folders List** displayed.

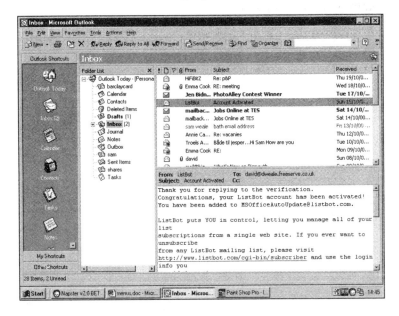

Preview Pane

The **Preview Pane** is normally shown in the bottom right-hand side of the screen where you can see or preview the contents of a message (see the screen above). This command toggles the pane on and off.

Auto Preview

Selecting this shows the first few lines of the messages in whatever view you are using. The screen below shows an example how this looks.

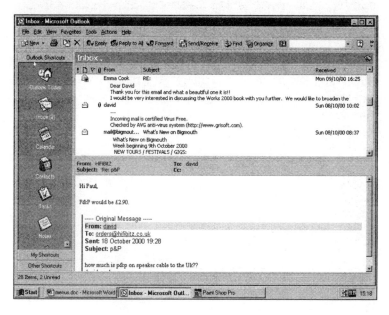

Expand/Collapse Groups

A group is made up of items with something in common for example the same person sent them.

If you group items then you can expand/collapse the group headings to display/hide the items they contain.

Creating groups

Pull down the **View** menu, select **Current View**, and then choose a view, e.g. **By Sender**.

Pull down the **View** menu, select **Current View**, and then **Customize Current View**. Finally, select **Group By** and choose how you wish to group the items.

Make any other choices you wish within the dialog box and return to the screen. The items should now be grouped and you can click the ⊞ and ⊟ symbols to expand or contract the display.

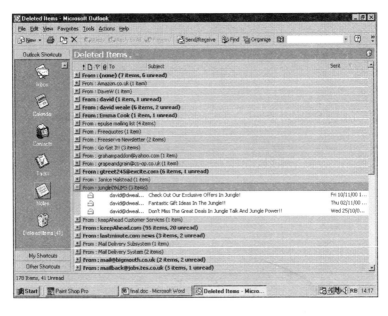

Toolbars

You can choose which toolbars to display, the **Advanced** toolbar is shown below.

It is also useful to **Customize** the toolbars.

Customizing the toolbars

One of the ways in which I customize my programs is by using this feature to remove toolbar buttons that I do not use very often and replace them with buttons I make use of.

Use the **Tools** menu; select **Customize** followed by the **Commands** option to do this.

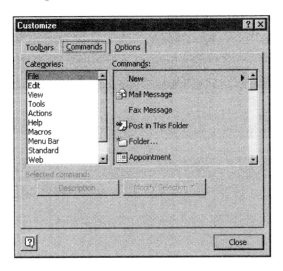

Adding buttons

To add new buttons, select them from this screen and drag them into position on to the (chosen) toolbar

Removing buttons

To remove existing buttons (you must have the window shown above open to do this), click the button and drag it off the toolbar.

Status Bar

The **Status Bar** appears along the bottom of the screen and displays messages e.g. how many items there are. This command toggles the **Status Bar** off and on.

Favorites menu

This menu is the same as the Favorites folder within
Microsoft Internet Browser and can be used in the same
way, e.g. adding favourites, organising the folders.

If you select any web sites within the folders, you will be
prompted to connect to the Internet.

Tools menu

Send & Send/Receive

An alternative to the **Send & Receive** button on the
toolbar, with the difference that **Send** allows you to send
messages without also receiving any.

If you have set up various e-mail accounts, you will be
prompted to select the one you want to use.

Address Book

Displays the **Address Book**.

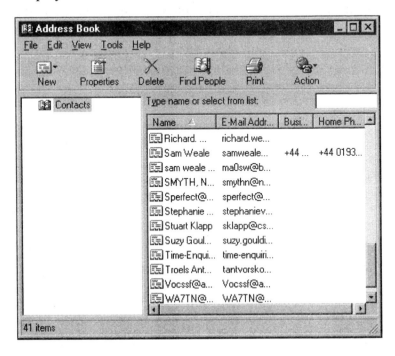

New

This button enables you to add a new **Contact** or **Group**.

New Contact

Select this to enter details of a new contact, enter the details including the e-mail address, and then click the **Add** button to add the e-mail address to the list.

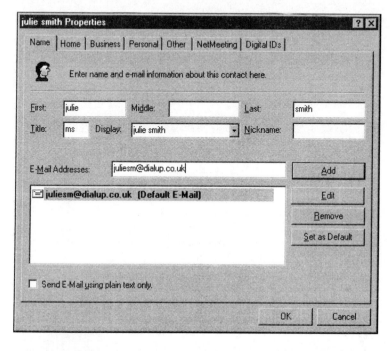

You can add other details using the tabs along the top of the dialog box.

If you need to change the e-mail address, click the **Edit** button.

New Group

The advantage of creating a group is that you can e-mail everyone in the group by selecting the group (instead of having to select every member of the group individually).

Select **New Group**, then enter the name of the group and select contacts from the address book (you can add new people using the **Add** button, however these will not appear in the address book itself, to add them to the address book use the **New Contact** button).

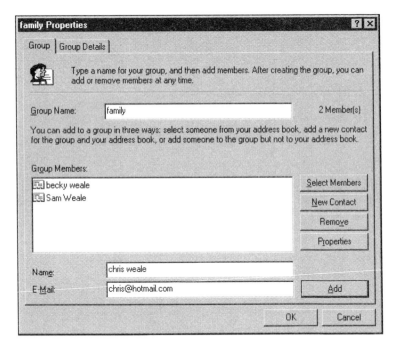

The new group will be shown as a folder within the **Contacts** folder.

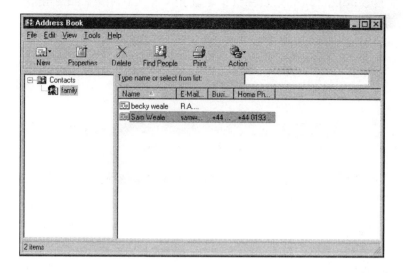

Find People

If you have a large address book, there is a possibility that you may need to find a contact within it.

Enter details in the dialog box and all the contacts with those details will be displayed.

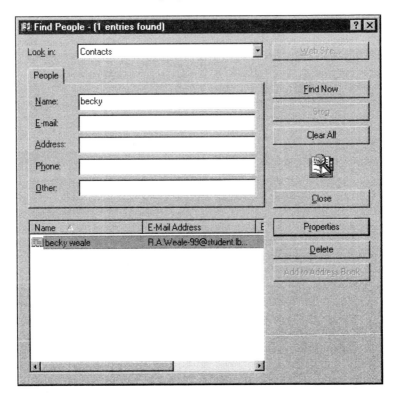

Action
Rather than having to return to the main
screen, you can use this button to carry out
several activities.

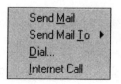

Find & Advanced Find

Displays the search boxes (described in another part of this
book); **Find** and **Advanced Find** enable you to look for
text strings within any **Outlook** items.

Organize

Similarly, this displays the **Organize** window.

Rules Wizard

You can create rules for dealing with your mail, for example, to move e-mails from a certain source to a folder (other than the Inbox) on arrival.

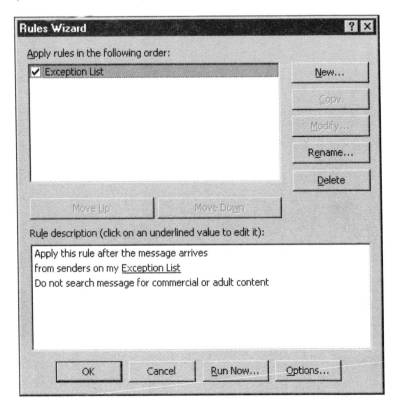

To begin this process, click the **New** button and you will be presented with several choices.

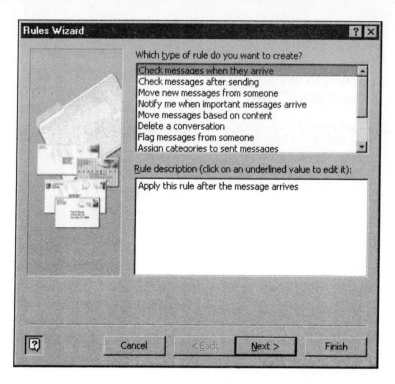

Rules Wizard

Which type of rule do you want to create?

Check messages when they arrive
Check messages after sending
Move new messages from someone
Notify me when important messages arrive
Move messages based on content
Delete a conversation
Flag messages from someone
Assign categories to sent messages

Rule description (click on an underlined value to edit it):

Apply this rule after the message arrives

Cancel   < Back   Next >   Finish

You select a rule (how the rule works is described in the lower half of the screen) and move on to the next screen.

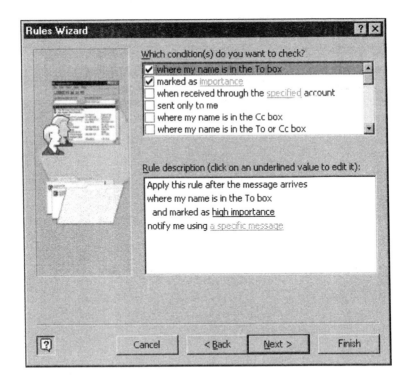

At this point, you can amend the actions contained within the rule.

You have to make decisions by clicking the <u>underlined</u> choices in the bottom half of the screen and then either adding text or selecting from a list, e.g. if you click *specific message* then you have to enter the relevant text.

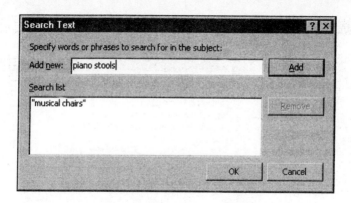

The following screen is for you to decide the action to take.

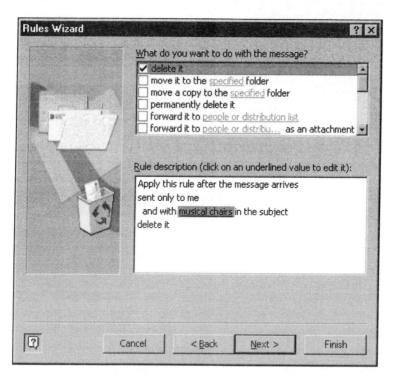

Then you decide upon any exceptions to the rule.

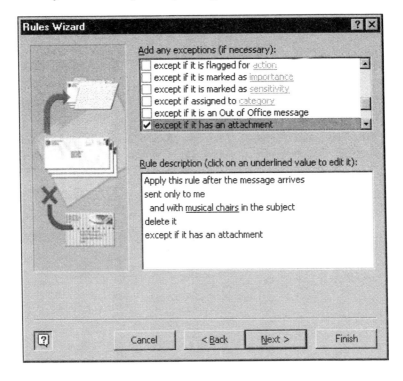

Finally, you name the rule and you have finished. The rule appears within the list of rules and you can modify it, delete it, or move it up or down the list.

Empty "Deleted Items" Folder

This deletes all the items held temporarily in the **Deleted Items** folder. There is a failsafe (just in case!).

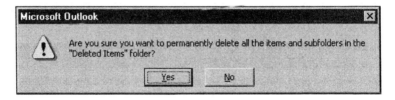

Forms

You can display any of the various forms or design your own new form (based upon an existing form) by adding text and fields.

This is a very powerful tool and one that can be used to create customized templates (which can be used instead of or alongside the original forms).

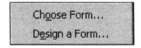

Choose a form

You can select from the list of existing forms and then open the form.

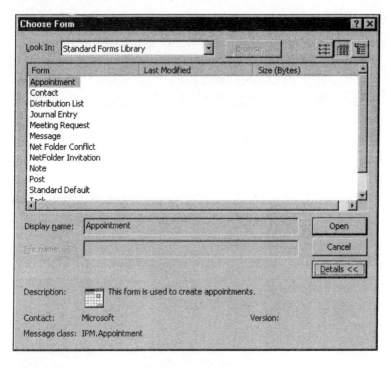

Note the **Details** button, you can click this to see an explanation of the purpose of the form.

Design a form

You can design your own form, beginning with an existing form and then adapting it to your own purposes.

Once you have selected the original form, it is displayed, and you make changes, add fields and save the form (by default it saves in the **My Documents** folder and to edit forms you have created, you need to pull down the list and select **My Documents** in the **Look In** list). The form is saved as an **.oft** format – the **Outlook Template** file type.

The example shown below is of a message form to which I have added two fields, **Due By** and **Created On**.

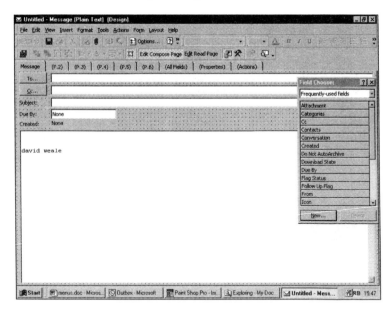

When you want to use a form or create another form, go through the same process (remembering that the forms you have created yourself are saved in the **My Documents** folder).

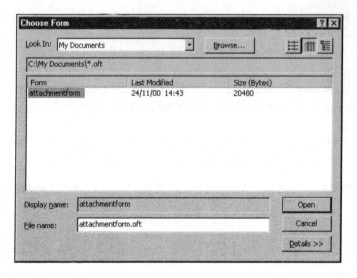

Below is the newly designed form in use; you can see that when it is actually sent the **Created On** box is automatically completed (the **Due By** field was filled in when I composed the message).

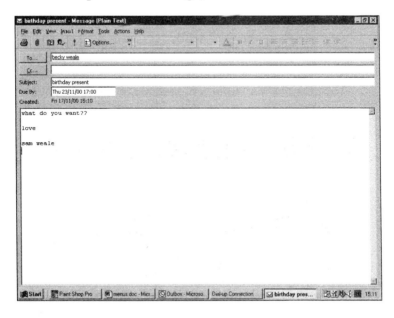

Macro

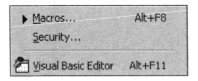

You can create macros to automate tasks, however you have to use **Visual Basic**.

(Macro) Security

The default setting is to allow you to decide whether to run macros that arrive in your mail.

You can change this although it is not a good idea to reduce the level of your protection.

As a matter of basic security, you should have an anti-virus program installed and running (and make sure it is up to date).

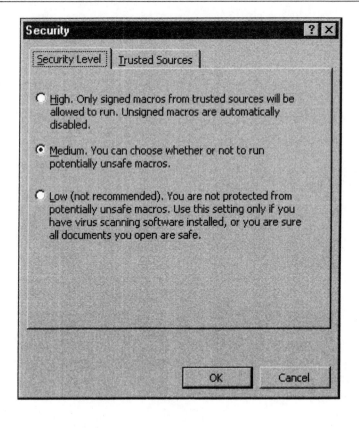

Accounts

This tool displays the mail accounts you have set up (or imported into the program).

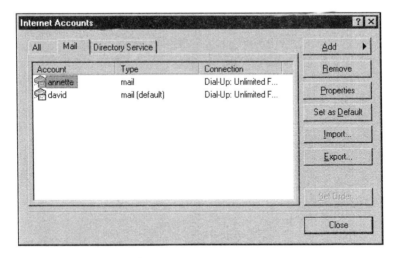

You can add new accounts, remove accounts and so on, please remember that to set up an account you need to know the precise details of your mail servers and your mail account details. An example is shown on the opposite page.

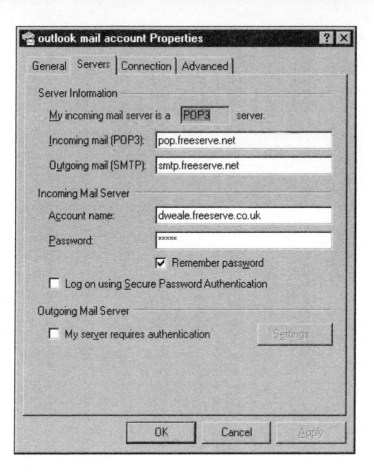

Options

This is where you can alter the way the program functions.

Each tab allows you to alter aspects of the program.

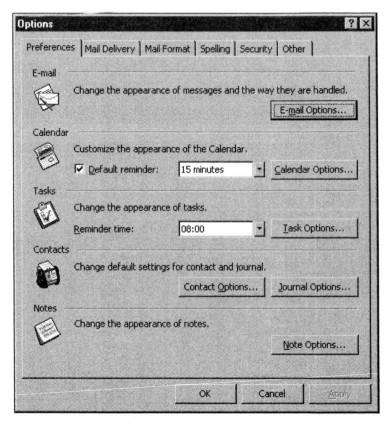

Initially, you may want to retain the default settings, however as you become used to the program, you may begin to consider changing these settings to suit your own unique situation.

Customize

Permits you to customize the program (more details appear in the section on the **View** menu).

Actions menu

New Mail Message/Fax Message

Similar to the **File** menu and the **New** toolbar button.

New Message Using

More exciting, this displays choices.

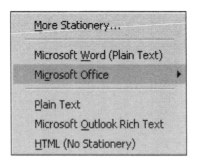

More stationery

A cornucopia of styles and images, you can select from these to add variety to your messages and if you use the **Get More Stationery** button, you connect to the Internet and can add more layouts.

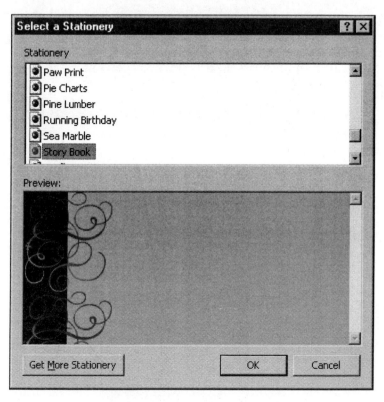

Microsoft Office

This loads the relevant application within the message.

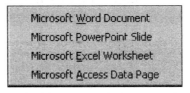

The illustration shows an **Excel** worksheet within the body of a message.

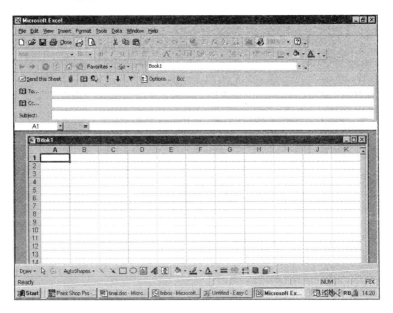

You can only send single worksheets, PowerPoint slides, etc., using this method. To send a complete file, include it as an attachment.

Flag for Follow Up

You can set a flag so that the message has the flag attached to remind you to follow it up.

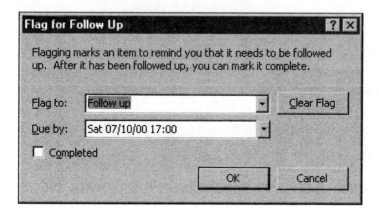

Find All

Finds messages using the **Find** dialog box.

Junk Mail

You select messages and add them to the following lists.

If you also set rules for **Junk** or **Adult** messages then all messages from these sources will be dealt with automatically.

Reply/Reply to All/Forward

Replicate the buttons on the toolbars.

Help menu

You can use the supplied help in several ways.

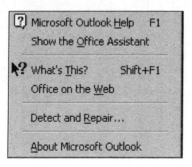

Microsoft Outlook Help

This activates the **Help** screens; these are very similar to all the Office 2000 help and contain several different ways of accessing help.

Normally when you first select this, the **Assistant** will appear, you type in a question, click **Search** and a list of alternative answers will appear. Choosing from this list displays the (normal) help screens.

To display the traditional help, click the **Show** button.

As you can see from the illustration, there are **Contents**, **Answer Wizard** and **Index** options.

Note the buttons along the top of the help screen; these enable you to move back or forward through the screens you have looked at or to print out the text.

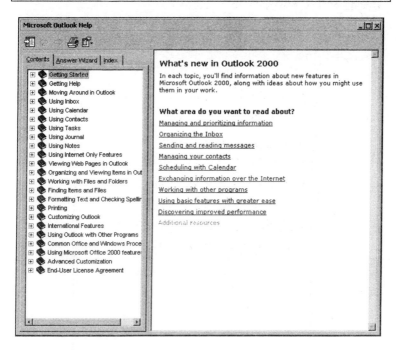

Contents

The contents are like a series of books or chapters on the various aspects of the program.

> Double-clicking on any itcm will reveal the sections within that book.

Answer Wizard

Instead of choosing from a list, here you type in the word or phrase and the nearest equivalents are displayed so you can select the one you want. The details are then shown in the right pane.

Index

This includes a list of keywords as well as the option of typing a keyword.

Show the Office Assistant

This shows the assistant, clicking it displays the search box where you enter your question and obtain a series of answers; you select the most relevant answer.

Office on the Web

This option will connect you to the Microsoft site on the Internet. Your browser (e.g. Microsoft Explorer) will be loaded and so will the site.

Detect and Repair

This option will, with the help of the original discs, fix problems in the installation of the program.

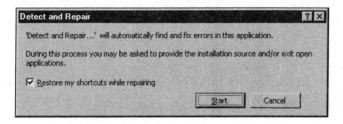

About Microsoft Outlook

This displays information about the program, for example the specific version number.

Index

Notes

Notes

Notes

Notes

Notes